Leisure Arts 38

Painting
Miniatures in
Acrylics

Cyril Turner

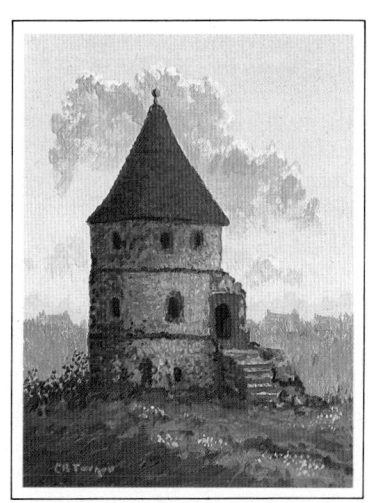

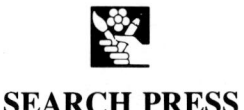

SEARCH PRESS

D0193182

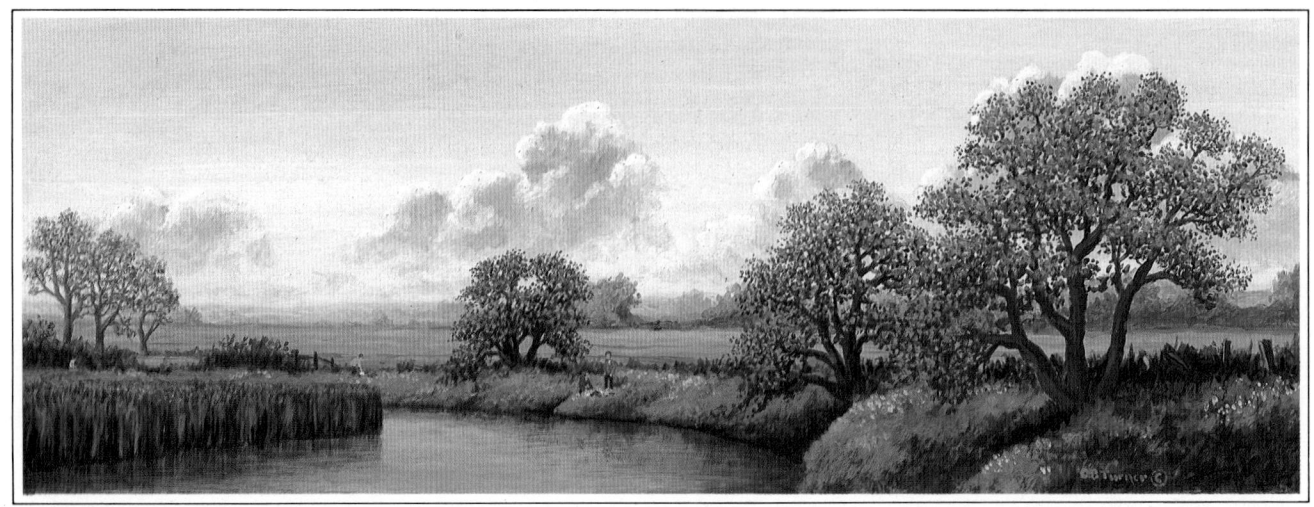

Stokesby, Norfolk (see pages 22–25).

Introduction

People have been painting miniatures for thousands of years. Throughout history tiny pictures have been created either as decoration or to illustrate religious themes. These miniatures are as popular today as they ever were. They are worked on a very reduced scale. The smaller they are, usually the higher the standards have to be to achieve such fineness of detail.

Whether you are an experienced miniature painter, or a complete beginner, the first thing you have to think about is the selection of your subject and the size and shape of your final painting. Just as for a larger painting the picture has to be well balanced and complete, and not just comprised of details extracted from a larger composition. Scale is the first consideration; composition and balance are important, and to a lesser degree overall size has to be considered.

There are many subjects which can be recreated in miniature – landscapes, still life, floral studies, buildings, portraits, animals, etc. I do not cover all the subjects in this book, but attempt to help you create a miniature painting using a variety of stage by stage demonstrations. By following these instructions, and studying the pictures, you will soon be able to confidently choose your own subjects and to capture them in miniature.

As with larger paintings, it is important to consider space as a part of your miniature. Subjects such as still life, floral studies, portraits, etc., require sufficient space around them so they do not appear cramped. Leaving slightly more space than is necessary makes little difference and retains balance, whereas slightly insufficient space is most noticeable and destroys the harmony of the miniature.

Once I have chosen my subject, I always make a sketch of the same size and shape as my intended miniature and apply artistic licence to balance the composition. There may be a need to leave some items out completely, or I may have to alter or adjust their position to make a more pleasing composition. Quite often I have to insert depth or distance into the picture. When working on a miniature scale artistic licence is far more easy to apply and is more flexible in its use.

The following demonstrations and stage by stage paintings have been planned to help you build up confidence in miniature techniques. By using this book and by practising, you will soon be able to choose and paint your own beautiful miniatures.

Materials

A variety of surfaces can be used with acrylics. These include Bristol board, paper, card, wood, glass, board, vellum. If you are a beginner, mountcard or Saunders mould made HP paper on board will provide a good base. The miniaturist can cut down most of these larger surfaces to the size required. It is worthwhile taking time to experiment by applying a complete background to your chosen surface. If you like the result, then carry on.

Acrylics are versatile and quick drying, and are an ideal medium for the miniaturist. If you do not have a 'wet' palette (see further on in this section), only put out a small amount of each selected colour, otherwise the paint will harden as it dries. A retarder can be added to the colours to slow down the drying process, if required.

I prefer to use a wide range of colours. I find that often a fine line of colour change is the best and easiest way to obtain some of the intricate detail in a miniature painting. As only small amounts of paint are used, your tubes will last for a long time.

Brushes should always be of good quality. I use a 1 cm (½ in) flat sable for backgrounds, areas of sky and water. For the main part of my painting, I use nylon brushes : nos. 0–1 flat and 000–1 round. Then for finishing off and fine detail, I use kolinsky sables nos. 00000–1 round; some of these brushes have a very fine point and some have a rounded point (spotting sables).

Various mediums are available for use with acrylics. I recommend that you use an 'acrylic flow improver', which helps to improve the flow of the paint on a base that is non-absorbent. I find by using this medium I can achieve a lovely even finish on my miniatures, which would be impossible otherwise. Gloss and matt mediums can be diluted and mixed with the paints. The colours either take on a glossy look, or their brightness can be reduced. I find the matt medium can be helpful on occasion.

I would advise that you use a 'wet' palette as acrylics dry so rapidly. I find an old dinner plate is ideal. Cut six layers of kitchen roll to fit, then place them on the plate. Wet the layers of paper thoroughly, remove the excess water, then place a piece of greaseproof paper over the top. Small amounts of paint can now be placed on the greaseproof paper, and they can be mixed on this surface using an old paint brush. The colours will not dry as long as the kitchen roll is kept moist.

I keep a sketchbook by my side for recording anything I find interesting, and always keep a few well-sharpened HB pencils available. Rubbers are not an essential part of my equipment, but if you do need to use one, make sure it is soft. Kitchen roll always comes in useful for mopping up – and glass jars make handy water containers. A watercolour palette filled with water and with two or three pieces of absorbent tissue in the bottom provides a useful way of cleaning brushes. The brushes can be rolled against the tissue without fear of damage, and the water can be used to clean off the paint.

Although I do not work with a magnifying glass, you may find this a useful piece of equipment. Some magnifying glasses can be bought complete with attachments and a light. When working under a magnifying glass it is important to remember that you must always have the centre of the glass over the area of the picture you are working on, as the edges of the glass can distort the view a little.

A viewfinder is another useful item. Different sizes and shapes of window can be cut out of a piece of card, to the same dimensions as your proposed painting, (oval, square or round, etc.). By holding the viewfinder not further than four inches away from you, and by looking through the aperture, you can work out and decide upon the composition of your painting.

I work on a drawing board and prefer to have it slightly angled. It is better to work in daylight if you can, but if you do have to work in artificial light, then cover your working surface with black card or fabric and place your miniature on top. The black background will prevent light from reflecting up into your eyes while you are working.

Framing

Once you have finished your miniature you will want to frame it. It is more appropriate for original fine art miniature paintings to be framed without a mount or matt. Therefore when selecting suitable shapes and sizes for the finished painting, you can take into account the selection of readily available stock sized frames as shown

Rectangular frames: 4.5 cm × 6 cm (1¾ in × 2⅜ in), 5 cm × 7 cm (2 in × 2¾ in), 6.7 cm × 8.6 cm (2⅝ in × 3⅜ in),

Oval frames: 5.5 cm × 4 cm (2⅛ in × 1½ in), 7 cm × 5 cm (2¾ in × 2 in)

Circular frames: 6 cm (2⅜ in) diameter.

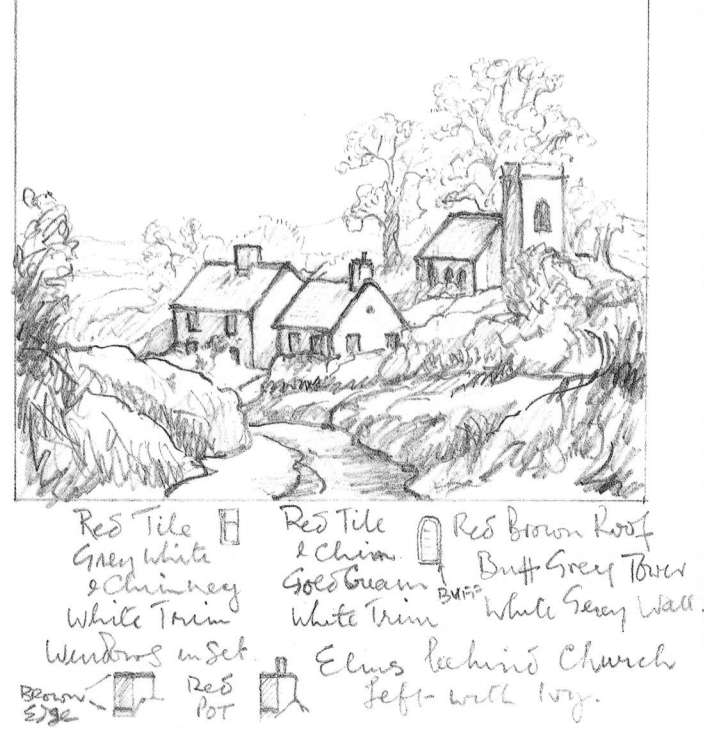

Master sketch showing rough notes

Techniques

Here I cover my methods of working, so you will be able to follow the stage by stage instructions in this book. By using these methods, and perhaps by eventually adopting your own as you progress, you will be able to choose subjects that appeal to you which can be captured in miniature.

I always work from initial sketches on my more complicated miniatures. When seeking inspiration for landscapes or outdoor scenes I often embark on sketching trips which can last up to a week. I easily get lost in my work for hours if I stumble across a suitable subject. When painting still life I often arrange studies. These arrangements do not always need sketches. However, it sometimes helps to make an outline sketch the same size as the intended painting.

The first thing I have to decide upon is the size and the shape of the painting. For a painting to be classed as a miniature it is becoming a more general practice now to reduce the image to less than a sixth of its actual size, (see the demonstration on page 10). This rule can be applied as a general guide when you are looking for a suitable subject.

When considering landscapes the size and shape is really determined by the content. If the view is panoramic, then I favour a longer, narrower format, (see page 2). If the view is more 'enclosed', then I prefer a more upright format, (see page 14). If the subject is still life or flowers, circular, oval or straight-edged formats can be used. It is up to you to study your subject

and decide on the best way to present it. Practise different formats and a few simple sketches in your sketchbook. The overall size of your painting should be limited in area to approximately two hundred and twenty five square centimetres (thirty six square inches), although this can vary depending on the individual miniaturist. The aim is to paint in the most diminutive scale which will automatically restrict the overall size. Ultimately, when viewing an original fine art miniature painting the actual overall size should contain three elements: depth (distance), light and space, and the whole work should present itself as complete, not bound by a frame.

4

If you are not happy with your subject, the painting can be improved by increasing either the distance, light or space within the picture. By doing this the working scale will automatically be reduced; often this enhances the miniature. Or apply a little artistic licence; move items around if the picture seems unbalanced. Leave them out or adjust them slightly. Work at the composition until you are pleased with the results.

When painting landscapes I always make notes to accompany my first 'master' sketch. Also, I draw any small details on a larger scale at the side of the first sketch, if I feel they will enhance the finished painting. When making sketches, although to your eye the pencil lines are black and white, try to imagine them in full colour. It is an interesting exercise and helps in the final analysis of the miniature. Colour notes are particularly helpful and I always add these to the master sketch.

Once I am happy with my master sketch, I draw out a simplified copy and split it up into areas as follows: 1 foreground; 2 middle ground; 3 middle distance; 4 far distance; 5 extreme distance. I use this sketch as reference throughout Stage 2 of the painting. Each area is worked on separately and it helps to bring a three dimensional effect to the finished miniature.

In the first stage, using both sketches as reference, I work on the background colours using a 1 cm (½ in) flat sable and a size 0 nylon brush, applying the paint with quick even strokes. The brush should remain moist at all times and should be cleaned at frequent intervals. If you choose to use a watercolour palette, (see page 3), the brush may frequently be gently rolled on the tissue under the water. This will keep it clean and undamaged. The whole working surface on to which a miniature is painted should be completely covered to form the background, and not left partly worked.

It is important to keep the base clean and dust-free throughout all stages of working. During the drying stages (there are three in each demonstration), I place the miniature in a dust-proof container and allow it to dry thoroughly before going on to the next stage. This is usually approximately three hours. But it is better if it is left to dry overnight.

During Stage 2, I explain how to build up the colours in all areas of the miniature using a variety of smaller sized brushes, (see 'Materials' on page 3). Rather than being specific in my instructions regarding which brushes I use in Stages 2 and 3, I feel it is better for you to practise using the various sizes on a separate piece of paper before applying the paint. Use small brush strokes, building up layers of colour with each brush, until you feel confident enough to attempt the next stages of your miniature.

Occasionally I use a stippling technique. For this I use one of my old paintbrushes, and I cut off half the hairs so the tip is 'blunt'. I then cover the area I am working on with one colour, and using a slightly darker shade I apply small amounts of the paint over the base colour, allowing it to peep through in places. This technique is a little difficult with acrylics because of its quick-drying qualities, but a retarding agent can be used to slow down the drying process.

In Stage 3 I demonstrate how to add the final colours and tiny details to the painting, which will enhance the miniature.

Wild roses: demonstration

Size: 6 cm diameter (2¼ in diameter)
Base: Bristol board (thick)

This demonstration is painted directly on to a prepared base from an arranged study, and therefore I would not normally use a sketch. However one has been made here to assist in scale reduction. Also it helps to achieve a balanced composition if you plan out your sketch beforehand.

Balancing a circular format is best achieved by first drawing in the area around the edge of the circle, and then positioning the remaining flowers and buds, without the foliage, in the central area.

I have used Bristol board as a base here because it is ideal for the sharp clean cut fine lines required on small formats. Also, I have applied the one sixth rule and reduced the roses to one sixth of their original size.

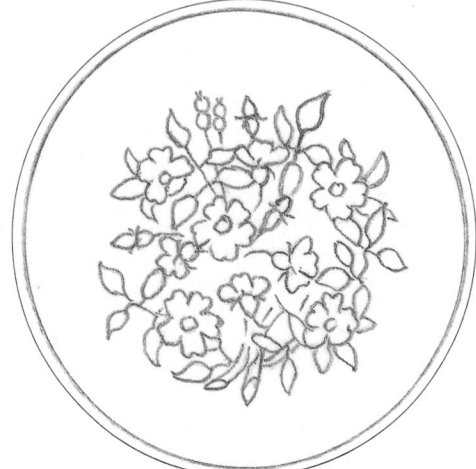

Outline sketch

Stage 1

Before starting, I check that the base is absolutely clean and free from dust. Then I completely cover it with a mid-blue background mixed from cobalt blue, Payne's grey, ultramarine and titanium white. This background is applied with a 1 cm (½ in) flat sable, using quick even continuous strokes across the base, which produces an overall even finish. I then place the painting in a dust-proof container and allow it to dry thoroughly.

Using a mid-grey and a size 00 kolinsky sable round with a very fine point, I carefully draw in all the outlines. Changing to a size 00 nylon round brush, I fill in the roses and flower buds using a mixture of titanium white with touches of yellow ochre and quinacridone red. Then I paint in the leaves, buds and stems using sap green, ensuring that all the drawn outlines are covered. The miniature is now left to dry.

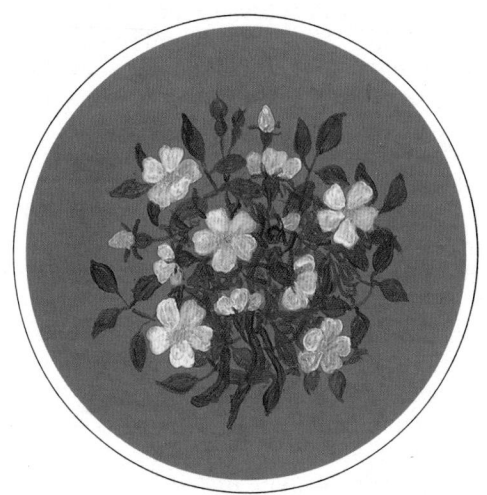

Stage 1

Stage 2

I mix three shades: a peach pink, a very light pink and an almost white pink from titanium white, naphthol crimson, quinacridone violet and yellow ochre. Using a size 00 nylon round brush, I work the roses, blending in these three shades, petal by petal, with brush strokes made towards the centre. I mix three shades – light, mid and dark from yellow ochre, raw sienna, red iron oxide and Mars black, for the centres of the flowers. I blend these in carefully.

I mix a variety of green shades from light to dark from sap green, chromium oxide green, permanent green, olive green, azo yellow medium, yellow ochre and Mars black. Then, using a size 00 nylon round brush, I work the leaves indicating areas of light and shadow. I add the main central veins and fill the centre of the painting with interwoven foliage. The miniature is now allowed to dry thoroughly.

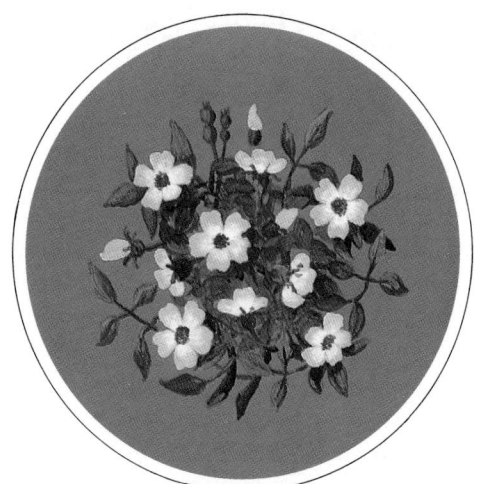

Stage 2

Stage 3 – the finished painting

I mix three shades of peach, pale pink and very pale peach for the flowers from titanium white, quinacridone violet, naphthol crimson and yellow ochre. Using a size 00 kolinsky sable round brush, I paint in the flowers exactly. I work on each individual petal blending them in from peach through to pale pink, and very pale peach towards the centres. With mixes made from yellow ochre, raw sienna, red iron oxide and Mars black and using a size 000 kolinsky sable round brush, I paint in the centres of the roses exactly. Changing to a size 0000 kolinsky sable round brush with a very fine point, I paint in the anthers as a series of placed fine lines with specks around the centres.

I mix a variety of green shades from very light to very dark, using sap green, permanent green, olive green, azo yellow medium, cadmium yellow light, yellow ochre and ivory black. Then, using a size 000 kolinsky sable round brush, I paint the foliage in and shape it up exactly. Working on each individual leaf, I place all the veins and the serrated edges. I paint in the stems exactly and strengthen shadows and highlights. Finally I carry out an overall check and make any slight adjustments or alterations to complete the miniature.

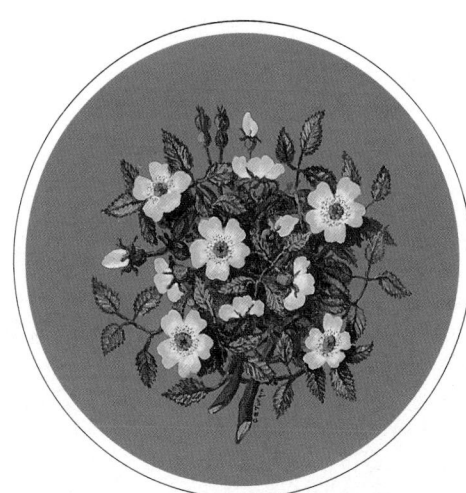

Stage 3 – the finished painting

Primulas: demonstration

Size: 6 cm × 4.5 cm (2¼ in × 1¾ in)
Base: Bristol board (thick)

Although a smaller format is used here than is used in most of the demonstrations in this book, the size is by no means small for a miniature. It is a popular size for most miniature categories, including landscape and portraiture, and I have applied the one sixth rule, reducing the primulas to one sixth of their original size.

First I make an outline sketch to help me with the scale, composition and picture balance.

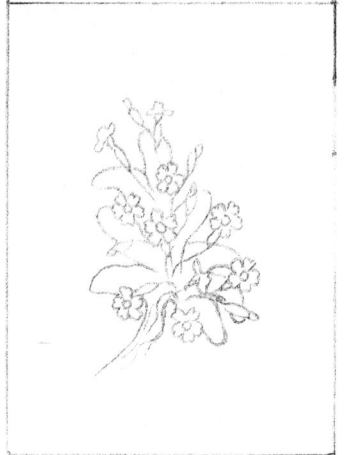

Outline sketch

Stage 1

All of the finer work on this miniature is carried out with a good quality size 00 kolinsky sable round brush. However, to start I use a 1 cm (½ in) flat sable. First I ensure that the base is absolutely clean and free from dust, then I completely cover it with a background mixed from titanium white, with touches of dioxazine purple, ultramarine and Payne's grey. I start at the top and work downwards, using the flat sable to apply the paint with even, continuous strokes across the base. I then place the miniature in a dust-proof container and allow it to dry thoroughly.

Once it is dry, I carefully draw in all the flower and foliage outlines, using a mid-grey. Then, with a mixture made from dioxazine purple and quinacridone violet, I fill in the flower petals. Using a mixture made from olive and sap green I fill in the leaves. I also place the sepals and flower stems using a mixture made from sap green and yellow ochre. I now leave the painting to dry for approximately one hour.

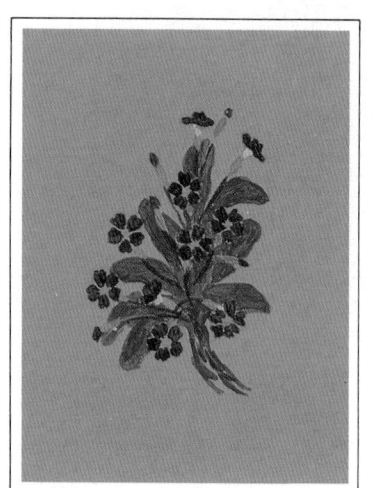

Stage 1

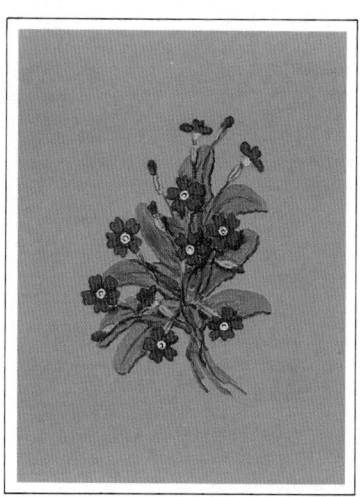

Stage 2

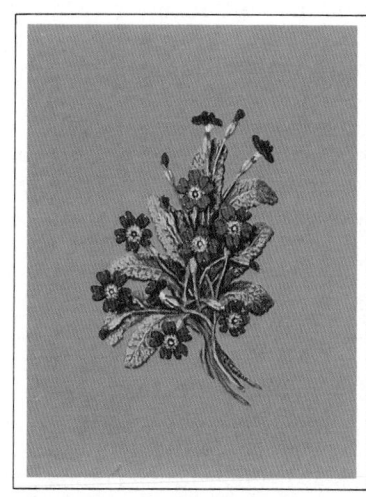

Stage 3 – the finished painting

Stage 2

First I mix three shades for the flowers, using dioxazine purple and quinacridone violet – light, mid and dark. For the foliage I mix a variety of light, mid and dark greens, using sap green, olive green, permanent green, cadmium yellow medium, azo yellow light, yellow ochre and ivory black.

Now I work each flower, blending the colours in, petal by petal. Brush strokes are made from the outer edge of the flower towards the centre. I paint in the small areas in the centre of the flowers using a dark brown mixed from burnt umber and Mars black. Then I paint in the yellow centres of the petals using cadmium yellow medium and cadmium yellow light. I place each stigma using azo yellow light. I use a light greenish yellow for the light underside of the petals and the sepals.

I shape up the leaves and place the main veins using burnt umber. Finally, I line in the flower stems more clearly using burnt umber. I now leave the painting to dry for approximately one hour.

Stage 3 – the finished painting

Continuing with the same colours, I make mixes to cover the entire range used for the foliage. First I place the two shades of deep shadow exactly. These are the areas of shadow caused by the flowers, which are to the right and below each flower, and the areas of shadow in the centre caused by the flower stems, and the overlapping and folded leaves. I then place the main leaf veins exactly. Next, I paint in all the lightest areas precisely. These are mainly stippled in, so that the areas not covered will represent the hairline veins. This will also give the leaves the correct texture. I now paint in the remaining areas of foliage exactly, with the mid-colours blending in from light to dark.

Continuing with the same flower colours, I make mixtures to cover the entire range used. I work each flower petal by petal, blending their colours in towards the centre, then paint in the yellow centres exactly, blending the colour outwards from the centre. I paint in the buds exactly and also the sepals and stems, adding contrasts of light and dark to lift the interwoven stems away from the leaves. Finally I check the miniature closely and make any adjustments or alterations that are required to complete the painting.

Anemones

Size: 6 cm × 4.5 cm (2¼ in × 1¾ in)
Base: Bristol board (thick)

The subject matter for this miniature is arranged on a glass table top and painted directly on to the base, without referring to a sketch. I use the one sixth rule, reducing the anemones down to one sixth of their original size.

First I cover the background, using the same colour and techniques as used for the 'Primula' demonstration opposite (see Stage 1). Then I outline and line in the flowers, buds, stems and the foliage adjacent to the flowers using quinacridone red and olive green and a size 000 round nylon brush.

Using a mixture of quinacridone red and naphthol crimson I work on the flowers and buds, building up the colours and highlighting the centres and edges of the petals. I fill in the flower centres using a dark brown.

Finally I work on the remaining foliage, painting it in and working from the centre towards the edges of the arranged study. I use the same greens as for the foliage in the 'Primulas' demonstration opposite.

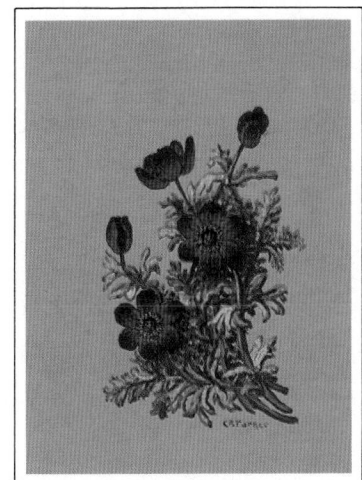

The finished painting

Antiques with tulips, fruit and miniature landscape: demonstration

Size: 11 cm × 8 cm (4¼ in × 3¼ in)
Base: Saunders HP paper on board

With still life studies it is not normally necessary to make a sketch of the subject matter, as these miniatures can be painted straight on to a plain base from arranged studies. However, it may be helpful to make an outline sketch the same size as the intended painting so the

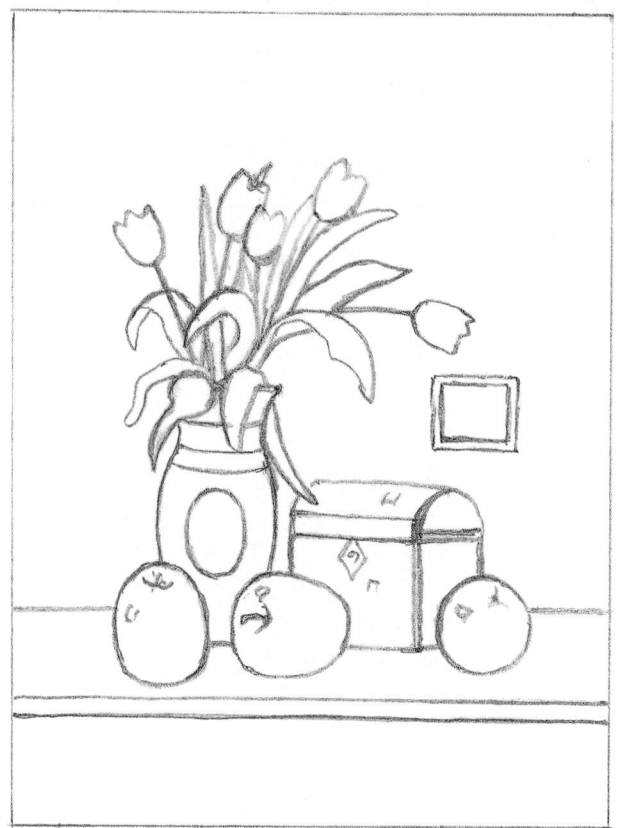

Outline sketch

overall uniform scale, composition and picture balance can be worked out beforehand.

As all original fine art miniatures are painted on a very reduced scale, the one sixth rule is applied as a general guide. At first you may find this difficult to judge. An easy way to achieve it is to measure one of the items you are going to paint. For example, in this study the antique tea caddy measures 12 cm (4½ in) across, therefore it should measure less than 2 cm (¾ in) across in the miniature. By drawing the tea caddy in first to set the scale, all the other items can be drawn in relative to it. This will result in a uniform scale of reduction throughout.

I arrange the items in the still life group, paying particular attention to the colours which can be a valuable aid when working on the perspective in a picture. The light grey background gives the best three dimensional colour combination. The pale gold ochre coloured frame of the miniature painting sets it in the background against the light grey of the wall. The blue of the vase and the brown of the tea caddy bring the two items forward in the picture. The same applies to the green and red of the tulips. The orange contrasts well with the brown tea caddy and the red of the apples stands out against the vase and the tea caddy. The bright colours of the fruit make them appear nearer.

Before starting, I position a light to give good contrasts of highlights and shadows. These highlights may be drawn in on the outline sketch for future reference.

Stage 1

I check the base material to ensure it is absolutely clean and free from dust, before covering it with a light grey mixed from titanium white and very small amounts of ivory black, cobalt blue and dioxazine purple. I apply it with a 1 cm (½ in) flat sable, using quick even continuous strokes across the base. I then allow the painting to dry thoroughly.

Using a size 00 nylon round brush with a very fine point and a mid-grey, I outline all the items. It is advisable to draw in the objects that stand above the back line of the table top slightly smaller, allowing for final adjustments if necessary, bearing in mind that the drawn lines will be covered at a later stage. Care should be taken when lining in the tulips. Once I have lined in

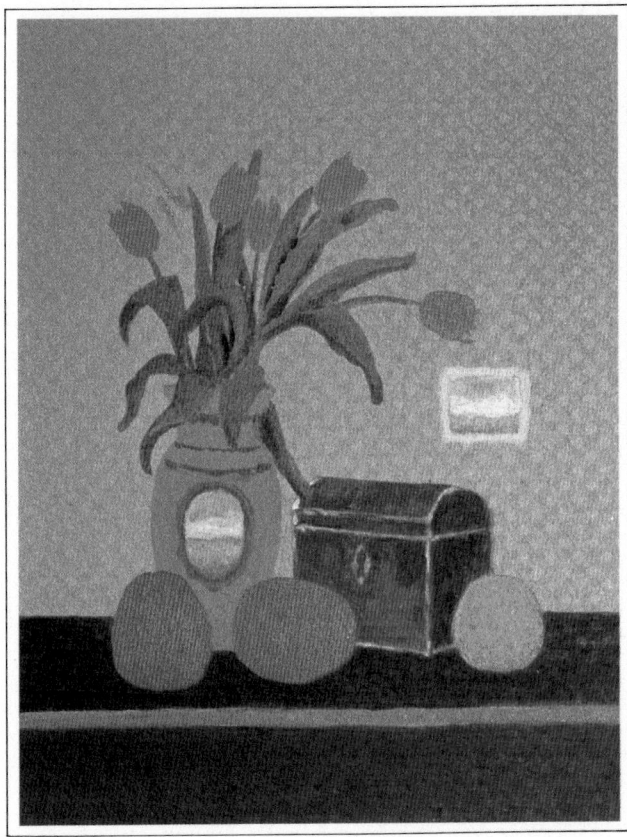
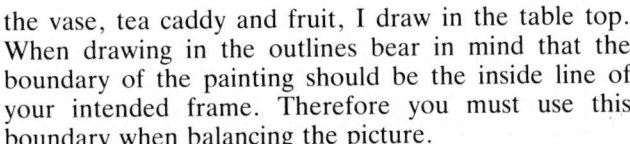

Stage 1

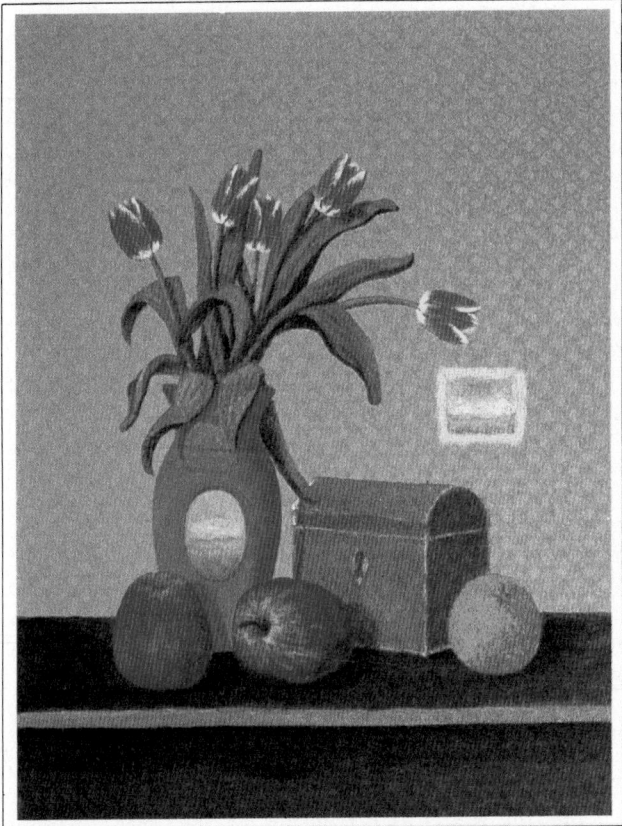

Stage 2

the vase, tea caddy and fruit, I draw in the table top. When drawing in the outlines bear in mind that the boundary of the painting should be the inside line of your intended frame. Therefore you must use this boundary when balancing the picture.

Using a size 0 nylon round brush, I paint in the vase using a mid-blue mixed from titanium white, cobalt blue and ultramarine. I place dark lines around the upper portion. Now I paint in the oval design on the vase and the miniature painting on the wall: a very light blue is mixed from titanium white and ultramarine for the top portions of each; I paint in the lower portions using light green oxide. These colours form the base for the two tiny landscapes.

I paint in the yellow ochre miniature frame and the

oval frame around the vase design. Using brown mixed from burnt umber and ivory black, I paint in the tea caddy and add light edging and the keyhole plate. I paint the table dark brown, which is mixed from burnt umber and Mars black, and add a light table top edge. Using a mixture of raw umber and cadmium orange I paint in the orange and then place the apples and tulips with a neutral base, red and green. I now leave the miniature to dry thoroughly.

Stage 2
First I check to ensure the surface is clean and free from dust. I work on all the items in this miniature separately, starting with the tea caddy which is the farthest away in the group. I mix browns for this using titanium white,

raw sienna, raw umber and Mars black, and paint them in showing light and shadow, leaving the detail work until a later stage. I work the blue vase next, mixing three shades of blue from titanium white, ultramarine and cobalt blue. I place the darkest shade on the areas in shadow: down the right side, to the right of the apple, and below the leaf on the left. I paint in the remainder of the vase using the lightest blue, painting over the dark lines around the top of the vase; these should remain just visible through the light blue. I line in the edge of the oval exactly and use the mid shade of blue to blend in the other two shades of blue down the right side of the vase.

I mix a range of colours for the tulips, including the greens for the leaves, using dioxazine purple, quinacridone violet and red, titanium white, azo yellow medium, light green oxide, sap green and ivory black. I paint in the tulips exactly, adding all the details. It is advisable to work on the flowers to a finished stage, except for the highlights, while they are still fresh and before the blooms open further. I line in the leaves and paint them in more precisely. Next I mix the colour for the orange and paint it in indicating the shadows; I place the stalk and line in the area around the stalk.

I mix a number of shades from dark red to yellowish green for the apples, using naphthol crimson, quinacridone red, permanent green, cadmium yellow light and dioxazine purple. First I work on the apple on the right, placing the stalk and painting in the area of light greenish yellow around it. I shape up the remainder of the apple and blend it in using mid to dark reds, indicating the shadows. Then I work the other apple, painting in the core and blending it in with the greenish yellow. I place the red shadows. Finally a very dark brown is mixed from Mars black and burnt umber. This is used to place the shadows on the table top and below the table top edge. Now I allow the painting to dry thoroughly.

Stage 3 – the finished painting
I mix browns for the tea caddy and table using titanium white, raw sienna, raw umber, burnt umber, burnt sienna and Mars black. Then I shape up the tea caddy exactly and add the wood grain. I paint in the ivory keyhole plate exactly and place the two main highlights and also the highlights around the edges.

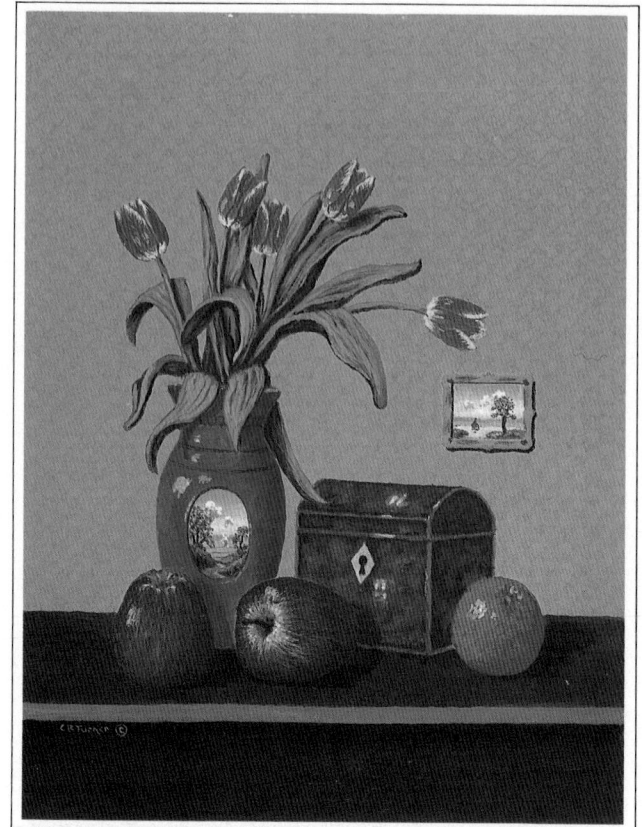

Stage 3 – the finished painting

I strengthen the dark blue lines around the top of the vase with a mix of cobalt blue and Payne's grey, then place the highlights on the vase using a mixture of titanium white, ultramarine and cobalt blue.

I shape up the tulip leaves exactly and adjust the shading. With mixtures made from light green oxide, azo yellow light, sap green and Hookers green, I blend in the lighter colours and I add highlights to the tulips with a mixture made from titanium white, quinacridone red and violet.

Next I square up the miniature frame on the wall and paint it in exactly, using mixtures made from yellow ochre, cadmium orange and raw umber. I place the shadow to the right and below the frame using Mars black.

I strengthen the colour of the orange and blend in more detail around the stalk, then I place the highlights. Now I finish, adding detail to the apple on the right. I lighten the area around the stalk with a greenish yellow which is blended in and placed exactly. I brighten the red slightly and paint in the main highlights, also the smaller highlights around the stalk. Next I work on the apple on the left. I blend in light red on the left and around the core, and paint in the main highlight on the left and those around the core.

I square up the table showing the shadows exactly, by making the table top edge slightly lighter. I add the two small landscapes, working both together. Mixtures for the clouds are made from titanium white, yellow ochre, indo orange red, ultramarine and Payne's grey. I place the skylines and distances using light blues with a very pale green placed directly below. Using mixtures made from light green oxide and cadmium yellow I place the marsh greens on the oval, then paint in the water area on the rectangle using light blue. I place the path using light and dark fawns and green, and paint in the windmill using red, brown and white. I paint in the tree and reed beds on the rectangle using greens, yellows and browns and place the yacht using red and browns. Finally I make an overall check to see if any slight adjustments or alterations are required.

Follow the techniques in the previous demonstration and the stages on the back cover and complete the miniature.

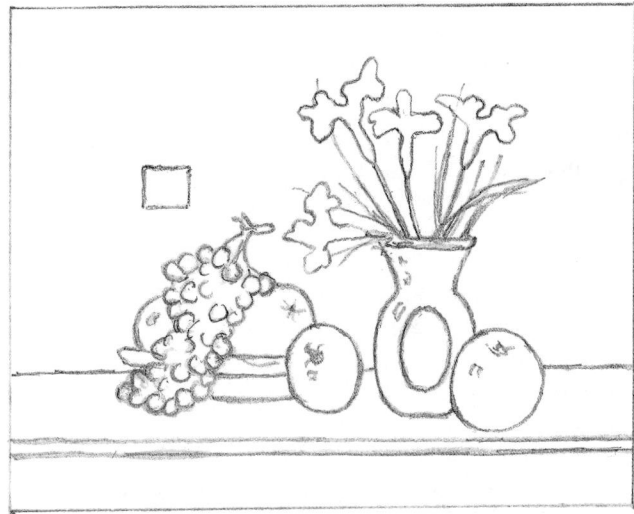

Outline sketch

Red glassware with fruit, flowers and miniature

Size: 7 cm × 8 cm (2¾ in × 3¼ in)
Base: Saunders mould-made HP paper on board

I do not go into any detail here with this still life study, as it is similar to the previous one opposite. The two intermediate stages can be seen on the back cover and the same principles and techniques are used as described opposite to produce the finished miniature.

First I draw an outline sketch, then I apply the background colour, using a stippling technique, (see page 5), to produce an unusual colour blended wallpaper effect. Then I add the other items.

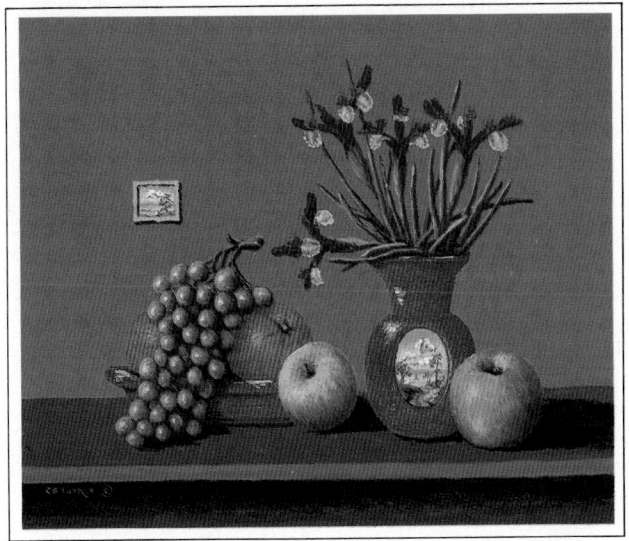

the finished painting

Killin, Scotland: demonstration

Size: 11.5 cm × 9 cm (4½ in × 3½ in)
Base: Saunders mould-made HP paper on board

Distance, light and space are not only found in the open, panoramic views of the following pages, they are also found in more complex 'enclosed' landscapes, such as the demonstration on these pages. Here the distance can be seen in the faraway hills and mountains. The light comes from two main sources. It comes from the sky which is somewhat restricted, but the extreme distance also gives some degree of light, and the other main source is the reflected light from the water running from the bridge through to the foreground area. There is considerable space in this painting; its composition produces a channelling effect which extends space through the entire picture to the area of extreme distance. This space can be found above the water running under the bridge and beyond; there is space along the length of the bridge, and also within the hills and mountains.

First I draw the master sketch the same size as my intended miniature, than I make a simple copy and mark in the areas 1–5 (see page 5 and above).

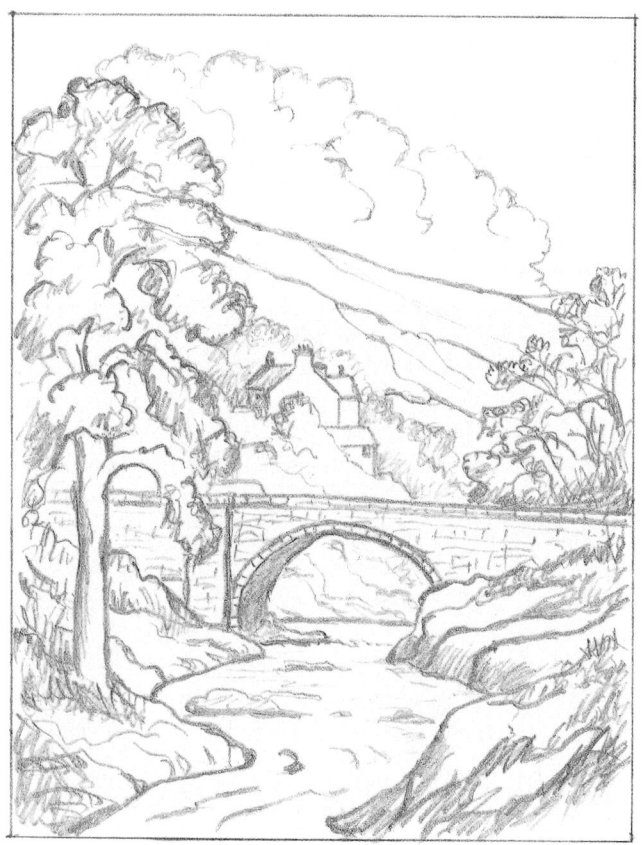

Master sketch

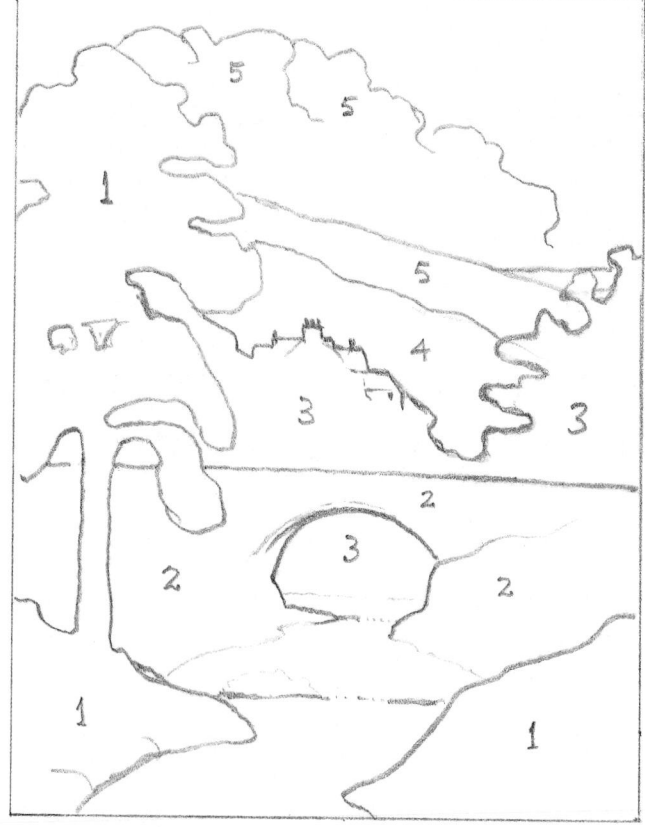

Area sketch

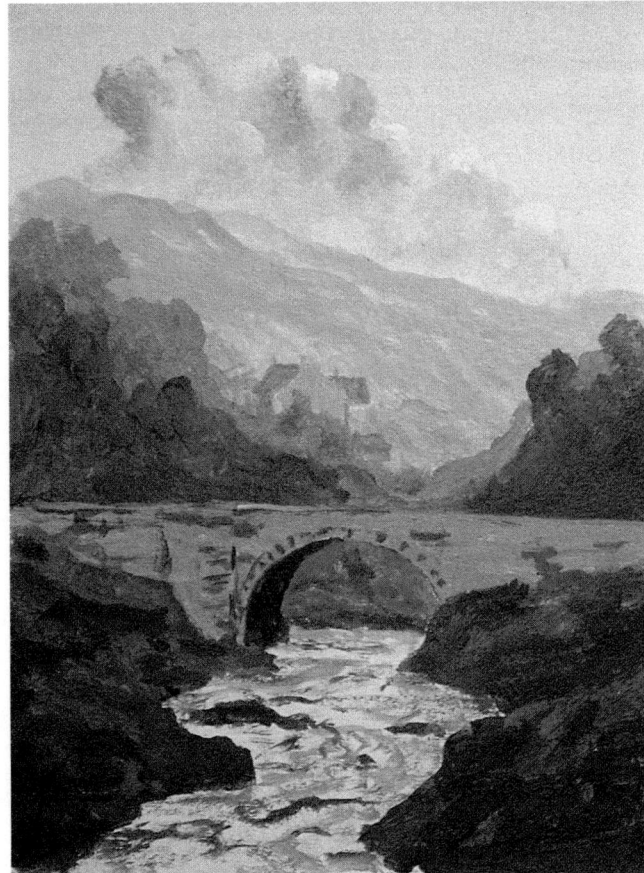

Stage 1

Stage 1

I mix the sky and water colours using titanium white and cobalt blue, making two light blue shades; one of these is very light. With a 1 cm (½ in) flat sable and using quick even continuous strokes, I paint a 2.5 cm (1 in) band of the darker shade across the top of the base; covering the area below with a 2.5 cm (1 in) band of the lighter shade. I paint the water in the foreground area in with the darker shade and the remaining water area with the lighter shade.

Next I mix another darker blue and a number of light greenish blues and light greens for the areas of extreme and far distance, using titanium white, ultramarine, light green oxide, azo yellow light and raw umber. I want to fill the area of extreme distance, so I paint it in using the darker blue shade. Then I use light greens and greenish blues for the far distance. Now I paint in the clouds using colours mixed from titanium white, ultramarine, Payne's grey and ivory black.

I roughly place the houses in the middle distance giving them buff walls and mid-grey roofs and paint in the trees in the middle distance using colours mixed from yellow ochre, cadmium yellow medium, olive green, Hookers green and sap green.

I work the middle ground area and start by drawing in the outlines of the bridge using a mid-grey. I mix colours for the bridge using titanium white, raw umber, ivory black and burnt sienna. A number of browns and greens are mixed from burnt sienna, ivory black, raw umber, yellow ochre, cadmium yellow medium, sap green and chromium oxide green; then I fill in the remainder of the middle ground. I paint in the foreground rocks and line the water, then allow the miniature to dry thoroughly.

Stage 2 (*see overleaf*)

Throughout this stage, each area is worked separately using the area sketch opposite as a guide.

Extreme distance (5): I mix the colours for the clouds and extreme distance using titanium white, Payne's grey, ultramarine, ivory black, yellow ochre and cadmium red light. I shape up the clouds exactly and blend them in, lightening their top edges. I lighten the clouds in the extreme distance down to the skyline, making the skyline and area of extreme distance softer by applying a very light blue in places.

Far distance (4): The colours for this area are mixed from titanium white, raw umber, light green oxide, phthalo green, azo yellow light and yellow ochre. I paint in the far distance and fade the hills falling away from the left into the extreme distance, blending the colours together carefully.

Middle distance (3): I mix a range of colours for this area from Payne's grey, raw umber, burnt umber, titanium white, raw sienna, chromium oxide green, sap green, olive green, cadmium yellow medium, yellow ochre and ivory black. I line up the houses and paint them in more clearly with blue-grey roofs and buff walls. I shape up the trees behind the houses exactly, and make those just to the left of the houses darker. I use light and

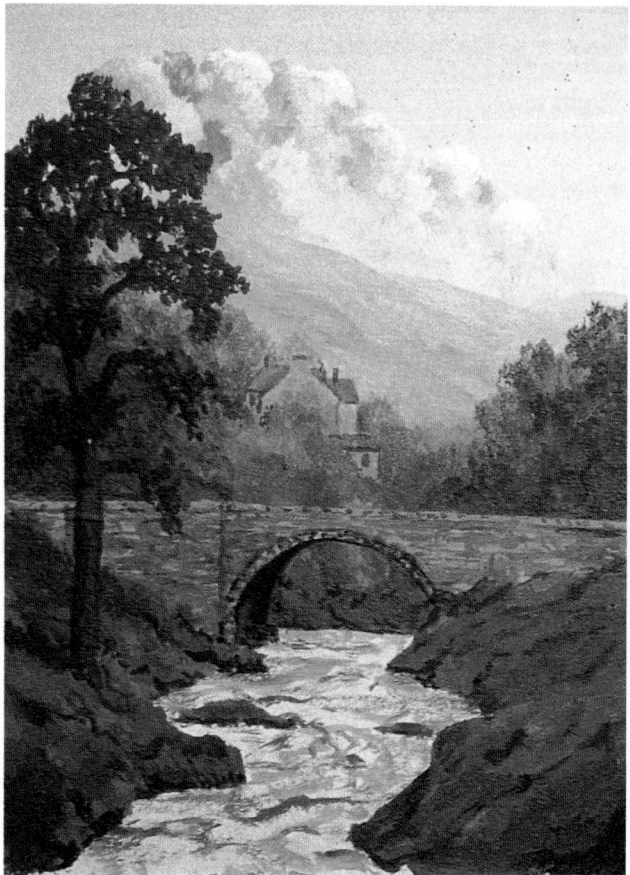

Stage 2

mid-greens and browns for the trees and foliage in front of the houses and mid and dark greens for those going upwards and to the left. I line in those on the right of the picture and under the bridge arch in more detail and paint them in using mid and dark greens and browns.

Middle ground (2): I mix a number of colours for the bridge and rocks from Payne's grey, raw umber, titanium white, ivory black, raw sienna and burnt umber. I line up the bridge exactly and paint it in more clearly, showing stone work around the arch and along the top. I add more detail to the rocks on both sides of the water so they are more clearly defined and paint in the grass banks using mid and dark greens.

Foreground (1): I line up the rocks on both sides of the water exactly and paint them in more clearly. I place the grass using mid and dark greens and paint in the Scots pine trunk and branches. I roughly place the foliage using a dark green. No work is done on the water during this stage. The miniature is now left to dry thoroughly.

Stage 3 – the finished painting

The miniature is treated as a whole during this stage. I highlight the top edges of the clouds with titanium white and blend in the body of the cloud with a mixture of titanium white, dioxazine purple and Payne's grey. A number of greens and browns are mixed from Payne's grey, raw umber, titanium white, raw sienna, chromium oxide green, sap green, olive green, burnt umber, cadmium yellow medium, yellow ochre and ivory black.

I blend in the foliage behind the houses exactly, and paint in the blue tint to their right, also blending in the foliage in front of the houses and under the bridge arch with more detail. I add branches and foliage to the trees on the right using light to dark greens.

Next I mix the colours for the bridge and rocks using raw umber, burnt sienna, burnt umber, raw sienna, Payne's grey, dioxazine purple, titanium white, ivory black and Mars black. I work the bridge and shape it up exactly to show details of the stonework, especially around the arch and along the top edge. I paint in the underside of the arch exactly.

I line and shape up the rocks exactly, adding light areas and shadows, and paint in the Scots pine trunk and main branches exactly, adjusting the foliage and showing full detail with light to dark greens.

To mix colours for the water I use phthalo blue, ultramarine, olive green, raw umber, titanium white, ivory black, chromium oxide green and Mars black. I place the area of water, starting with the darker areas at the bottom of the picture, and work along the sides towards the bridge. I paint in the light area on the other side of the bridge. Following the direction of water flow, I blend in the remaining areas, indicating the movement of the river with ripples and white broken edging. The grass areas on both sides of the miniature need shaping up and at the same time I paint in the flowers. Finally, I paint in the three figures on the bridge and the one on the right bank.

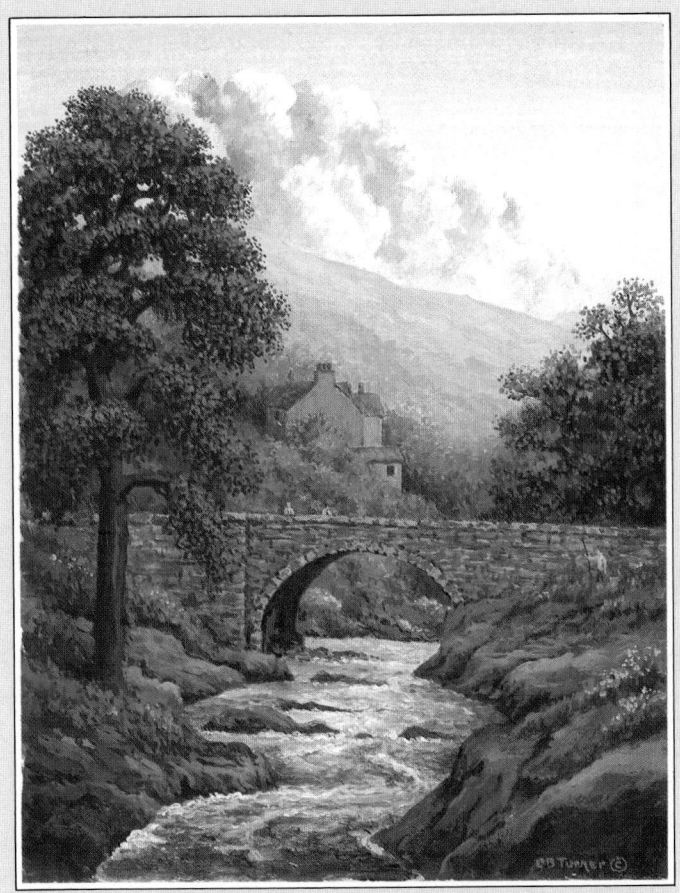

Stage 3 – the finished painting

Reed cutter's hut, Norfolk Broads: demonstration

Size: 6.5 cm × 18 cm (2½ in × 7 in)
Base: Vellum

Panoramic landscapes can be captured beautifully in miniature, as shown in the finished painting on page 21. The distant points are over eighteen miles away and the width of the picture in the background takes in a span of twenty five miles.

Once I have found the scene I wish to paint, I draw a master sketch the same size as my intended miniature (see below). First I draw in the foreground. Everything else in the picture is relative and you will find it fairly easy to fill in the remaining details.

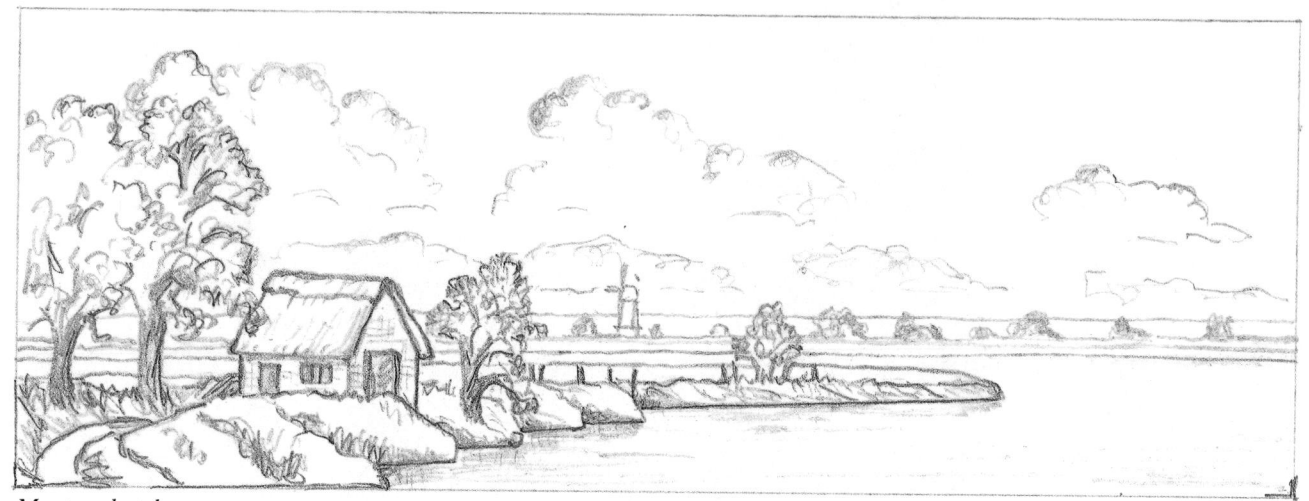

Master sketch

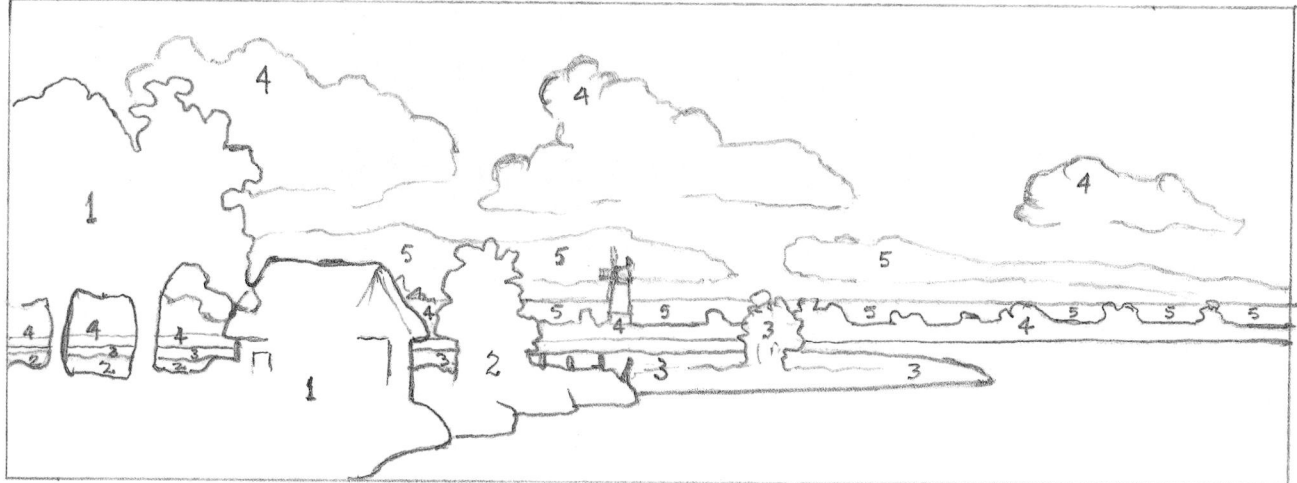

Area sketch

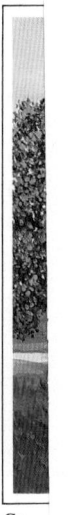

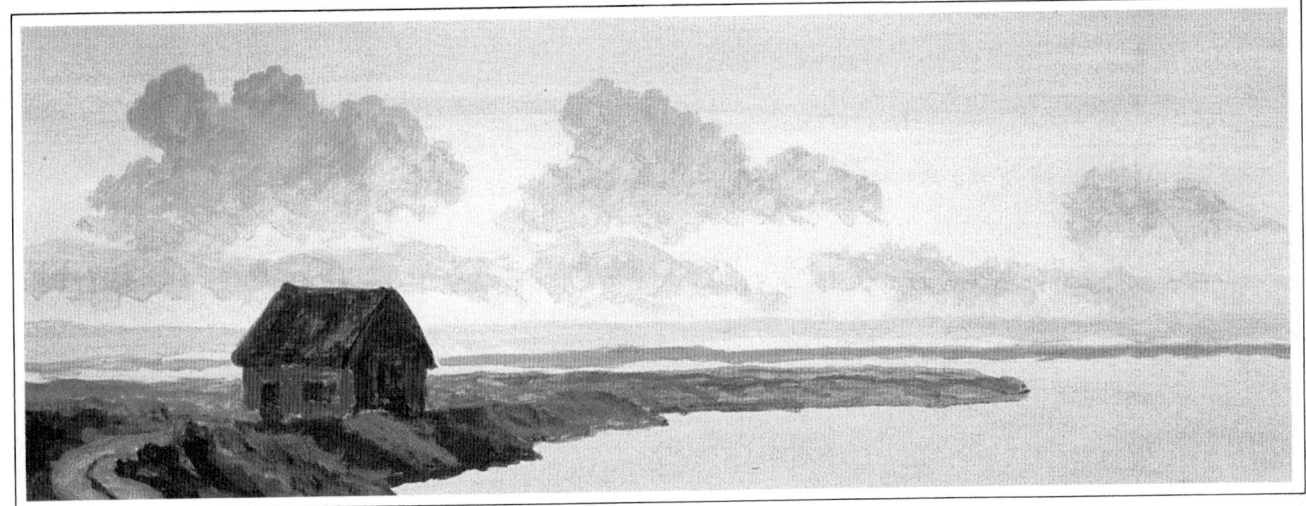

Stage 1

Stag

Stage 1

I then make a simple linear copy of the first sketch as shown and split this up into five areas ranging from the foreground to the far distance (see page 5). I am now ready to start applying the colours.

Stage 1

For the sky I mix two shades of light blue using titanium white with touches of cobalt blue and ultramarine. I then mix two shades of light peach using titanium white with touches of yellow ochre and indo orange red, increasing the amount of indo orange red for the darker shade.

With a 1 cm (½ in) flat sable and quick even continuous strokes, I paint in the light blues across the upper part of the vellum, placing the darker shade of blue at the top. Below these I apply the lighter of the peach shades overlapping it slightly and then I apply the darker peach shade down to the skyline. The different shades of blue and peach automatically blend into each other creating the feeling of distance as the darker blue fades away into the lighter peach.

With a size 0 nylon flat or round brush, I place in the main clouds using mixtures of ultramarine, Payne's grey, ivory black and titanium white. I position them carefully so that the overall picture balance is maintained. I ensure that they are in scale with the rest of the painting so they appear to move across the sky.

Next I paint in the area of water running across the middle distance, the middle ground and foreground areas on the right. I mix a light blue (titanium white with touches of cobalt and ultramarine) and apply the colour using a series of quick even strokes which run parallel with the bottom of the base.

For the area of extreme distance below the skyline, I use a size 0 nylon flat brush. I mix a slightly darker blue than that used for the water, using titanium white and ultramarine. I run the colour across the entire picture placing a lighter thin line below.

Next I paint in the area of far distance; this is the thin 'line' running across the miniature between the extreme distance and the water line. I apply light green which is mixed with titanium white and light green oxide.

The middle distance is filled with light and mid-greens, and the foreground banks are made up of darker greens. So I mix a number of green shades, from light to dark, using green oxide, chromium oxide green, sap green, olive green, Mars black, yellow ochre and cadmium yellow medium. These are painted in to represent the grassy banks of the river.

Mixtures from burnt umber, red iron oxide, cadmium orange and Mars black are used to paint in the reed cutter's hut and pathway, taking note of light and shadows. The painting is now left to dry thoroughly.

church tower and place them more clearly using light and dark greens. Extra care should be taken when working on items which stand above the skyline, because even the smallest of errors will clearly be visible.

Middle ground (2): I mix colours for the church, cottages and road from titanium white, Payne's grey, raw umber, red iron oxide, cadmium orange, yellow ochre, ivory black and Mars black. I line up the church exactly and paint it in using light and dark buff greys, indicating areas of shadow. I paint in the roof more definitely, using a rust red.

I line up the near cottage roof and chimney and paint them in with a rust red, indicating the shadows. I paint in the walls with an off yellow, line up and place the windows and add the shadows. I line up the remaining cottage roof exactly and paint it in with a slightly darker rust red. I line up the chimney and walls exactly and paint them in using an off white. I line up and paint in the windows and place the shadows.

Using a very dark green, I paint in and place the area of shadow between the church and nearest cottage roof. I paint in the area of foliage next to this shadow which runs from the rear cottage wall to the front of the church, using a very light green and brown. Finally I paint in the foliage area to the left of the farthest cottage using very dark to mid-greens.

Foreground (1): I shape up the road exactly and paint it in indicating the shadows and dark central area. I shape up the bank and bush on the left of the road exactly, with the addition of very light and mid-greens and browns. Using dark and mid-greens I paint in the foliage on the bush. I shape up the hedgerow and bank on the right of the road exactly and paint them in using very dark to mid-greens and browns.

Stage 3 – the finished painting

I mix colours for the clouds from titanium white, yellow ochre and indo orange red, then strengthen the top edges, adding highlights to their tips. With a mixture of titanium white, dioxazine purple and ultramarine, the main body of the clouds are blended in.

I mix a variety of very light to very dark greens and browns using cadmium yellow medium, yellow ochre, azo yellow light, cadmium orange, olive green, sap green, Hookers green, chromium oxide green, raw

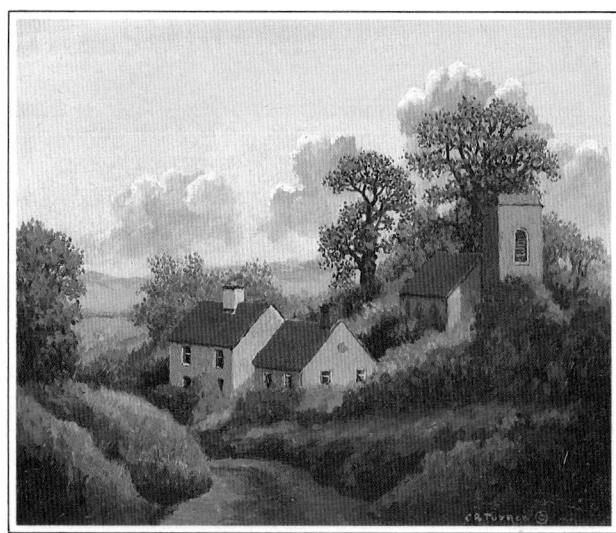
Stage 3 – the finished painting

umber, burnt sienna and ivory black. Then I work the two trees behind the church, painting in the trunks and main branches exactly and extending the branches slightly. I add the foliage, including the ivy on the left tree. Adding foliage and shading, I paint in the trees to the right of and in front of the church tower. I complete the bushes behind the left cottage using a mottled effect to show texture. I make mixtures for the church, cottages and road from titanium white, yellow ochre, Payne's grey, raw umber, ivory black, raw sienna, red iron oxide, indo orange red and burnt umber.

More detail is added to the church. I square it up exactly and place the window, shaping the roof as I work. Then I square up the two cottages exactly and add the window detail. More contrast is needed on the area of shadow to sunlight between the church and cottage, so I strengthen this and also lighten areas of foliage in direct sunlight. I darken the area of shadow to the left of the white cottage and work the bank on the right together with the hedgerow. The hedge has some browns added to its base and I place the foliage exactly. I shape up the left bank exactly and add highlights to give more of a contrast. I place the bush on the left bank more precisely and add foliage. Finally I lighten the road slightly on the left side and paint in the dark centre.

Old coach inn, Norwich: demonstration

Size: 13 cm × 8 cm (5 in × 3¼ in)
Base: Saunders mould-made HP paper on board

Buildings make interesting subjects for miniature paintings. This coach inn is a simple subject, but it is possible to choose buildings that are extremely complex.

It depends upon the amount of work you want to put into your miniature. I have chosen this subject because it is free from exact measured lines, which means the miniaturist can relax a little, and not be so precise in his approach. This, however, is not evident in the final painting where all the details are carefully painted in.

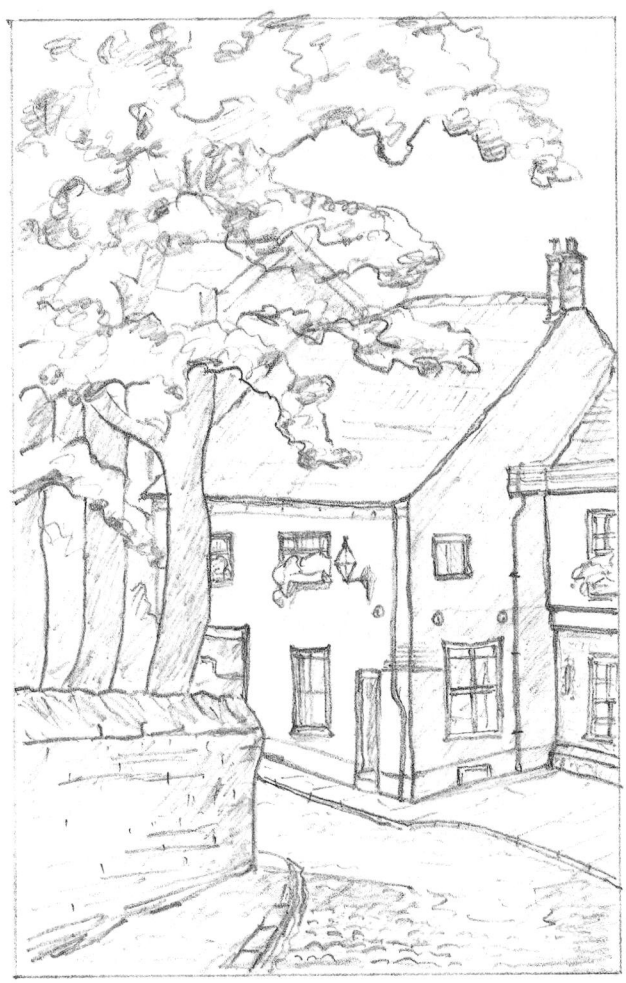

Outline sketch

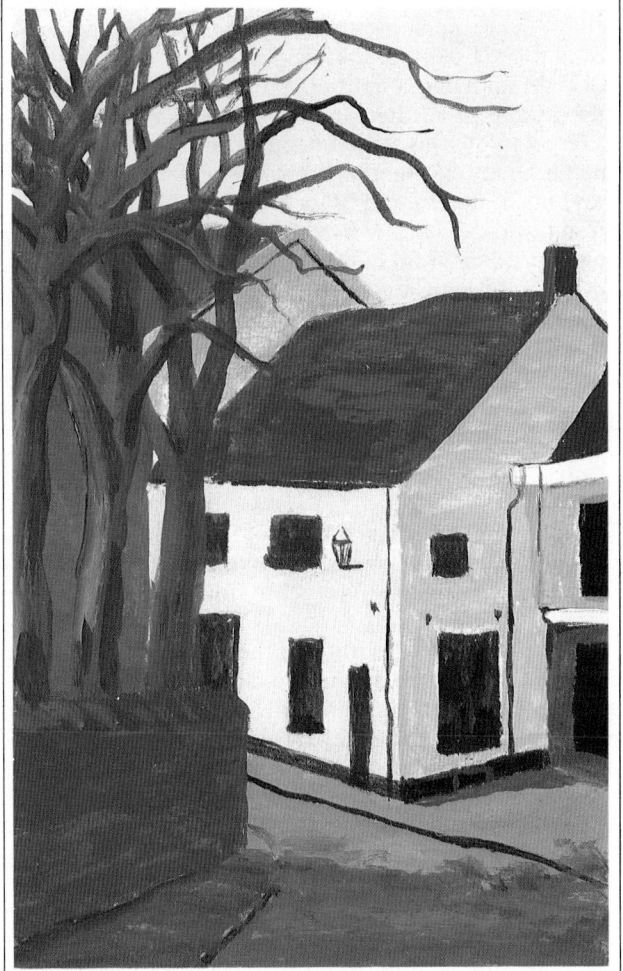

Stage 1

Stage 1

Using mid-grey and a size 00 round nylon brush, I draw in the outlines of the buildings, wall, pavements and tree trunks.

I mix a light blue for the sky using titanium white and ultramarine, and paint it in with a 1 cm (½ in) flat sable, using quick even continuous strokes across the base.

Next, I mix two shades of rust brown from red iron oxide and burnt umber, and paint in the roofs, chimney and wall. I use a mid-grey made from titanium white and Payne's grey to fill the end of the building on the left. Using two buff shades mixed from titanium white, yellow ochre and raw umber I paint in the inn walls. Using pink, I paint in the top portion of the building on the right applying a light cream strip above and below, then I paint in all the windows using Mars black.

To complete this stage I need to mix a number of light and dark greys using titanium white, raw umber, Payne's grey, burnt umber and Mars black. I use the lightest of these to fill the far pavement, and the darkest to fill the near pavement. I fill in the lower portion of the building on the right with a mid-grey and paint in the roadway which is not in shadow using a light brownish grey. Now I place the three tree trunks and main branches, painting them in with dark and mid-greys. I paint in the remaining areas with a mid-grey and leave the painting to dry thoroughly.

Stage 2

I mix a number of light to dark shades for the roofs, chimney and wall using red iron oxide, burnt sienna, raw umber, raw sienna, yellow ochre, olive green and Mars black.

First I work on the roof on the left, lining it up and blending it in. I line up the roof and chimney of the inn exactly and paint them in showing the basic details. I place the chimney pots exactly and then paint in the roof on the right and the wall showing the details.

Using a mid-buff grey made from titanium white, Mars black and yellow ochre, I paint in the gable end of the building on the left exactly and place the barge-boards with an off white.

I mix a variety of cream to buff mixtures using titanium white, yellow ochre, raw umber and cadmium red light, and paint in the walls of the inn, indicating the basic details and shadows.

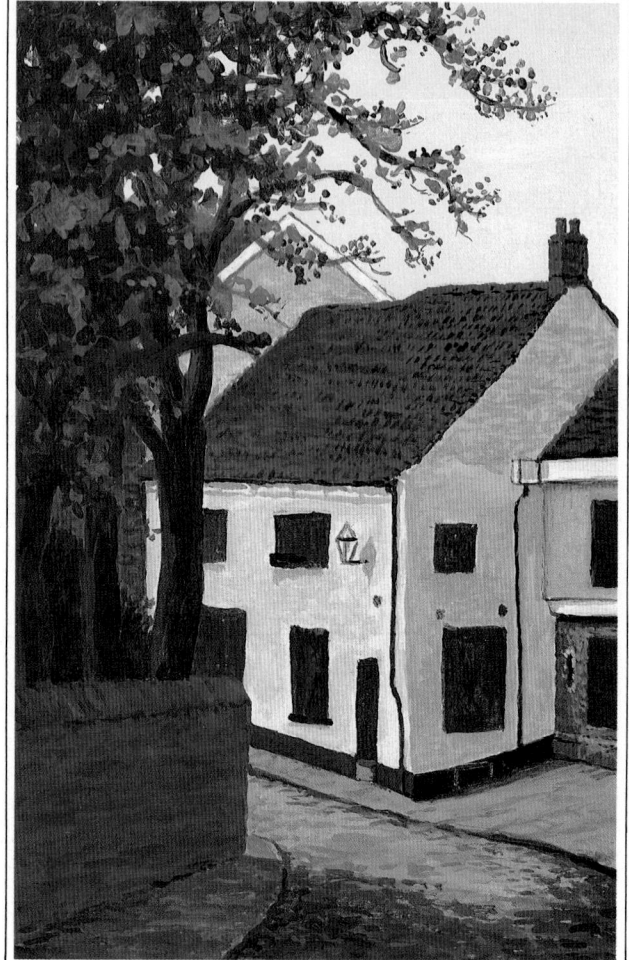

Stage 2

Next I mix a number of light to dark browns and greys using titanium white, raw umber, Payne's grey, burnt umber and Mars black, and roughly place the details on the pavements and road, indicating the shadows. I paint in the area behind the trees more precisely and place the tree trunks and main branches more exactly, indicating the shadows.

I line up the lower portion of the building on the right and paint it in more precisely, indicating the shadows. I line up the top portion and paint it in using a mixture made from titanium white and quinacridone red.

Finally, I mix a range of light to dark greens using sap green, olive green, Hookers green, yellow ochre and cadmium yellow medium, and roughly place the foliage. I now leave the painting to dry thoroughly.

Stage 3 – the finished painting

I make a variety of mixtures for the roofs, chimney and wall using red iron oxide, raw umber, burnt umber, cadmium orange, yellow ochre, olive green, Payne's grey and Mars black. I line up the inn roof and chimney precisely and place all the details exactly. I adjust the roof on the right slightly and place the lead edging using a mid-grey. I line up the wall precisely and paint it in showing all details, including the patches of moss.

I mix colour for the inn walls using titanium white, yellow ochre, raw umber and cadmium red light and line them up exactly, painting in the details and indicating the shadows and the underlying and corner brickwork.

Using mixtures made from Mars black, ivory black and burnt umber, I line up the inn windows, door frames, the downpipes, the circular support ends, the lamp and the black bottom surround and paint them in exactly.

I mix a number of light to dark greys and browns using titanium white, raw umber, Payne's grey, burnt umber, dioxazine purple and Mars black and paint in the inside of the inn windows exactly, placing in the reflections on the glass.

I line and paint in the pavements exactly, and adjust the cobbled road for light and shadow, painting it in exactly. I adjust the lower portion of the building on the right exactly for light and shadow, and paint it in exactly, adding the brickwork. I make the top portion of the building lighter, and line the beadings in exactly. Using off-white I place the window frames.

I adjust and paint in the tree trunks exactly, extending the branches to fall in front of the inn roof.

Finally I mix a range of light to dark greens using olive green, sap green, permanent green, yellow ochre, azo yellow light and Mars black. I extend the foliage and paint it in exactly. Using greens, reds and yellows I paint in the window boxes.

I give the miniature a final overall check, and make any slight alterations or adjustments as required.

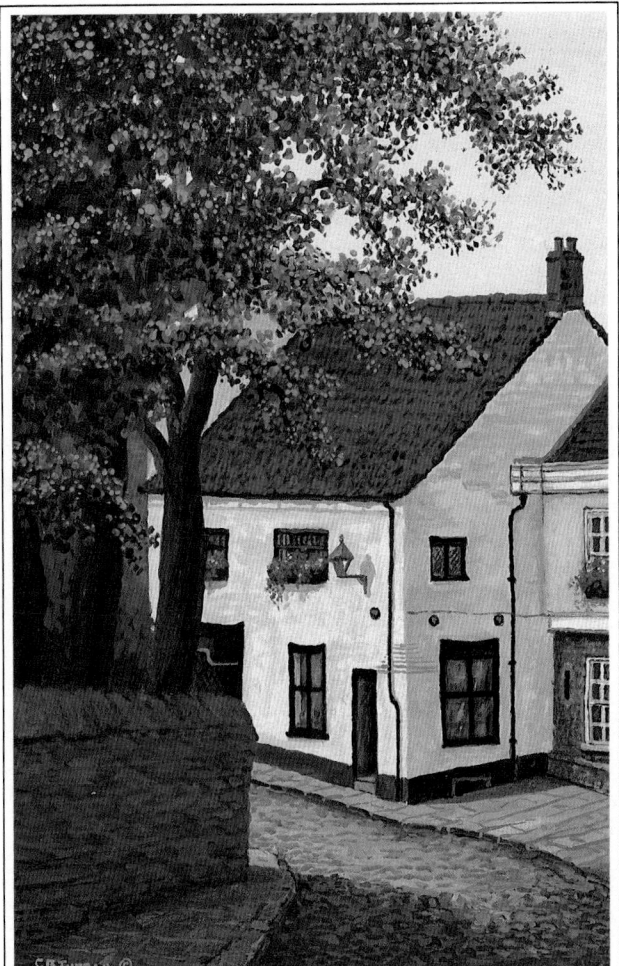

Stage 3 – the finished painting

First Published in Great Britain 1990
Search Press Ltd,
Wellwood, North Farm Road,
Tunbridge Wells, Kent TN2 3DR

U.S. Artists Materials Trade Distributors
Winsor & Newton, Inc.
11, Constitution Ave, P.O. Box 1396, Piscataway, NJ
08855-1396

Canadian Distributors
Anthes Universal Limited
341 Heart Lake Road South, Brampton, Ontario L6W 3K8

Australian Distributors
Jasco Pty. Limited
937-941 Victoria Road, West Ryde, N.S.W. 2114

New Zealand Distributors
Caldwell Wholesale Ltd
Wellington and Auckland

ISBN 0 85532 650 6

Laserset by Scribe Design, Gillingham, Kent
Printed in Spain by Artes Graphicas Elkar, S. Coop.
Autonomia, 71 - 48012-Bilbao - Spain.